Lifeguard Your Legacy:
What every Arizonian should know about Estate Planning

By Heidi J. Thompson, Ed.M, JD

Phoenix, Arizona
United States of America
2020

Acknowledgements

Most people don't like to plan for emergencies. It is a sad reality that estate planning may be the best procrastinated task of a responsible adult. Part of this is the dark subject matter (death and incapacity). But part is for lack of clear, easy-to-digest information. My hope is that this book will meet that need.

As it takes a village to raise a child, it takes a business network to write a business book. I'd love to introduce my readers to anyone in this list who might help you find success as you build your legacy.

To my clients – some of you have inspired these stories. Thank you for taking a chance on someone newer to the industry and for having the tremendous foresight to plan ahead when it is easier to procrastinate. It is my hope that your influence will clear the path for many more to take the estate planning journey.

To Josh Dorcey – thank you for dragging me--kicking and screaming--into a career that was both an easy fit and can grow with me. I wish you so much success in "the other" retiree's paradise.

To Stuart Gethner, my friend and real estate investment coach, for caring enough to make the introduction to Loral Langemeier.

To Loral Langemeier with Integrated Wealth Systems and my assigned Mentor there, Thomas Holland, and to my new friends and associates at Loral's Big Table – I can't wait to see what the year ahead brings for all of us and how this book might help us all find success in that process.

To Bill Walsh and Powerteam International, and particularly to Angel Tuccy – you gave me the confidence and design to get this book written and self-published on a very short timeline. I look forward to joining forces for some cooperative speaking soon!

To my NLN Gelie group – thank you for accountability hot seats: by making me put down dates for milestones, I had to get the book done. Who's next?

To my PMCC family (especially Jason Bressler), thank you for your introductions, business support, and care for our Phoenix community. You are my "hub."

To my WSRG ladies – you are amazing, classy, and fit my visual picture of success. Heather Guzman, that Periodization book made a huge difference in meeting this goal early. Thank you all for sharing, playing, and celebrating with me.

To the many other Phoenix meet-up groups (like SNP, Shakers & Stirrers, Networking REI, and Networking Phoenix events) - thank you for giving me the confidence in commercials, introducing me to people I needed to know, co-promoting on Facebook, and running easy-to-refer-to local businesses.

To my parents Stan & Marla – thank you for every imaginable opportunity and for the endless encouragement to live in the belief that I could do anything. You allowed me to dream. I love you more than all the green M&Ms in the world.

To my sister Becky – thank you for being my emotional coach, sounding board, occasional conscience, and constant friend.

To my daughter Sharayah – thank you for your laughter that breaks the tension, the shared puns, the interruptions that remind me what's important, the tea refills, and for the world's most beautiful grandkids.

To my son Chesney – thank you for living your best life and letting me live vicariously through yours, and thank you for singing with me.

To my grandkids Christopher and Cheyanne – though you can't read this yet, you are my biggest why (and my biggest fans).

To my husband Eric – thank you to saying yes to every crazy idea that I've dragged you into, for living so many chapters of adventures with me that we could fill 10 romance novels, and for continuing to dream with me.

To God – be glory for ever and ever, as every good gift comes from my Father above.

Legal Disclaimer

The information provided in this book does not, and is not intended to, constitute legal advice; instead, all content is for general informational purposes only. Information in this book may not constitute the most up-to-date legal or other information.

Readers should consult with an attorney to obtain advice with respect to any particular legal matter. No reader should act or refrain from acting on the basis of information from this book without first seeking legal advice from counsel in the relevant jurisdiction. Only your individual attorney can provide assurances that the information contained herein – and your interpretation of it – is applicable or appropriate to your particular situation. Use of this book or referenced resources do not create an attorney-client relationship between the reader and the author.

All liability with respect to actions taken or not taken based on the contents of this book are hereby expressly disclaimed. The content in this book is provided "as is;" no representations are made that the content is error-free.

Contents

Chapter 1: The Big Why

Do you squirm every time your Financial Advisor asks if you've done your estate plan yet? Let's face it, almost nobody wants to talk about the subject. We procrastinate. We make excuses. We don't want to do it, yet we want it done.

"Hope is Not a Strategy. Action is." This quote is a central theme shared by my friend, Chris Kempster, Managing Partner of Asset Protection Concepts.

He's right. In the world of wills and trusts there are high profile examples like Aretha Franklin and Prince who passed away without a will or trust. And the celebrities are not alone: about half of all Americans don't have even a simple will (and for those who do, many more are not current).

Failing to plan leaves family members waiting and hoping that the courts get it right, which leads to stress and fighting during a time that should be marked by togetherness and shared memories.

Ask someone who has recently updated their estate plan how they feel about it. Universally, you will hear themes of, "I have so much peace knowing it is done." It took action.

There is that nagging voice that reminds you that you really should just get it done. And you know that if you get those "affairs in order," you'll sleep better.

The voice gets louder every time you hear the horror stories about probate.

But somehow the whole idea is about as appealing as a tooth extraction.

It doesn't have to be like that. What if I told you that what we are doing is protecting your kids from being sued in a car accident?

Or protecting them from a failed marriage?

Or keeping your kids from fighting?

Or helping design a plan for the charities where you already volunteer?

Or maybe even taking care of Fido in the way that you've always pampered your fur baby?

Yes, we do that. And it is all relatively painless.

But hey...your best friend told you they just used a cheap or free online service to do their will or found a fill-in-the-blank form on Google.

It's a little like pulling your own tooth. You could do it. But what if it gets infected? What if you break the tooth? What if you damage the nerve? Chances are, the expense and pain of the cleanup is more than if you'd have just made the appointment to let the professional do their job. That's why you hear the horror stories.

Protect yourself from this avoidable self-inflicted pain.

Explore with me how you can look at your Financial Advisor this year with a happy nod that you've checked the estate plan off the list.

P.S. If you don't have a Financial Advisor, I can help you find the right one.

Chapter 2: Do I Need a Will or a Trust?

Probably the most common estate planning question is "Do I need a will or a trust?" It depends.

There are so many factors. The first is the state you live in. If you are in some states where probate is an absolute nightmare (like Florida or California), you need a trust. Case closed. The cost of a trust in these states is about 20% of the cost of probate. Money well spent.

In Arizona, I'd ask a few more questions because probate here is not the end of the world—and there is the possibility to avoid it without a trust if assets are well-structured.

Next I ask about your beneficiaries. Are they exceptionally good with money? If you leave them 50% of everything you have right now, would they manage it, invest it, and make it last toward the life you'd want them to have?

If the answer is yes, we might be looking at a will along with some asset planning. If the answer is no, we probably need a trust. Trusts allow us to create plans for distributions that are more detailed.

A trust also offers the possibility of protecting your children from divorce, creditors, and lawsuits. And a trust can give you some control over their lifestyle choices.

But a trust costs 3-4 times more than a will. This is partly because the document is more of a beast to draft and partly because it takes time to transfer assets into your trust.

Some clients are more concerned with guardianship than anything. Their children are still young. They just want to ensure that they've made the right arrangements so that if anything happens to them, the children go to a loving home with adequate provision. This might be a good place for a testamentary trust, which is a bit of a hybrid. It lacks some of the detail and a few benefits of a trust, but is generally no more expensive than a regular will. Remember that wills should be paired with good asset protection planning to avoid probate.

Customizing your plan involves some time in conversation. (Further proof for why using a cheap or free online service is less than ideal.)

Chapter 3: What Happens if I Don't?

As the saying goes, you may not think you have an estate. But you have an estate plan. It's called the state's plan. Do you trust the state with your estate?

Your Estate Will Go through Probate

There's a whole chapter later on probate. Probate is not the end of the world in Arizona. But someone has to do a lot of paperwork (often a lawyer), creditors get to stake a claim in your estate, and funds can be tied up for months with the exception of allowances.

In general, it will cost several thousand dollars, take several weeks of work, and take about six months to wrap up.

Putting this burden on family when it could be avoided with reasonable planning seems short-sighted (if not selfish). And the people you care about will be shouldering these duties during a time of grief, when they should be focused on comforting others with their fondest memories of you.

The Wrong People Might Get Your Stuff

Let's imagine that we were creating the laws for property.

We'd probably want spouses who have only ever been married to each other to give 100% of what they've earned to the surviving spouse. When the last spouse dies, we'd want the kids to equally split the estate. If there were no kids, we'd want any living parents to be next in line, followed by siblings, then by nieces and nephews, then aunts and uncles, then cousins, and so on.

For blended families, we'd want things just a bit different. Maybe half to surviving spouse and half to the deceased person's children.

Guess what? That's pretty much the way the laws read. When someone dies with a will, we call them testate. And without a will, we call them intestate. These laws that say who gets what when someone dies without a will are intestacy statutes. Makes sense, right?

However, maybe your family is not exactly like the Walton's. Perhaps you are living with a partner, but haven't chosen to be married. Or you've taken on responsibility for a family friend's daughter and are raising the child as your own. Unless there is a legal relationship, these intestacy statutes leave that person out in the rain.

And let's face it, there is probably someone in your family tree who you hope will never inherit your stuff. Your lazy-good-for-nothing brother. Your overly-entitled niece. Your substance-abusing child. Your weird, dog-hating uncle. The intestacy laws don't discriminate. The person with the closest relations gets her share at her turn unless you have a legal document stating otherwise.

You Might Not Get the Help You Need

So far, we've been discussing underground planning: wills and trusts. But there's above-ground planning, too. What if you were driving solo and got into a serious car accident? The ambulance identifies you, but you are not responsive. You're not dead, but you can't communicate. You are rushed to the hospital.

If you're married, they can call your spouse. But if you are single, you are now a ward of the state unless you have certain legal documents in place. The state is making your health care decisions until someone "claims" you with guardianship proceedings in court. This is costly and time-consuming. And completely avoidable.

In fact, if family members do show up at the hospital and there are no appropriate documents in place, the hospital legally can't even talk to family members about your medical status. Let that sink in for a minute. People you care about are sitting in the waiting room wondering if you are alive and the hospital can legally tell them nothing. And again: completely avoidable.

Will and trust packages include a Health Care Power of Attorney, Financial Power of Attorney, Living Will, and HIPAA waiver that can be so critical in times like these. It cannot be overstated how important it is to choose the person who should speak for you when you can't speak for yourself, handle your finances, and honor your medical wishes.

You Create Unnecessary Drama

In 1985, a hilarious movie, Brewster's Millions hit the theaters. Richard Pryor was brought into a lawyer's office to learn that a distant relative was leaving him a huge sum of money. He had to spend every penny of $30 million dollars in three days to inherit $300 million. This was much harder to do than he expected and the antics just got funnier. Coupled with his unique brand of physical comedy, I still think the movie is a must see.

But while will reveals are wonderful movie fodder, they are poor estate planning practice. I encourage my clients to share and discuss their will or trust. I even offer to facilitate family meetings, though very few clients take me up on this offer. By setting clear expectations, you can minimize later fights. You will uncover the objects that create emotional ties and division and reach solutions before it's too late.

Even worse than surprise will reveal is the unwelcome surprise that a loved one completely failed to create an estate plan. Don't trust the state to do it for you. And don't leave your family with uncertainty in their time of loss.

Chapter 4: The Whys?

Why Lifeguarding Legacies?

I use my Counseling degree more than my law
degree.

Before law school, I earned a masters in
Counseling and gained years of expertise in
counseling education. This may seem an odd
qualification for an attorney.

Yet much of estate planning is making a plan for
serving the unique needs of each beneficiary,
which requires some insight into developmental
needs. Some estate planning is focused on
finding solutions to avoid conflict between family
members, which involves predicting behavior and
emotional responses. Sometimes estate planning
requires mediation between two parents in a
blended family who have differing ideas of how
the kids should be supported. And sometimes,
estate planning involves sitting generations at a
table and explaining a complex plan. Counseling
is a significant part of the job.

Many attorneys who chose a career in estate
planning are more "transactional" in their
approach—that is, they push a few buttons and

most of their trusts come out with very few variations. They are a fantastic resource when it comes to business planning and asset protection, but they are not always thorough on the family and behavior planning side.

And if you've sat with attorneys, you know we have our own language. It takes skill to be able to take complex legal ideas and communicate them in a way that doesn't create instant migraines. With my many years in education, I can break down complex ideas with simple explanations.

Teaching is still a passion. I welcome the chance to talk to just about any audience for any length of time. I'm helping the Arizona Bar lawyers with better engagement techniques so that they don't just stand up and read PowerPoints. In my workshops, I break people into groups, ask lots of questions, and use fun pictures to seal in key themes and ideas. One talk I gave was to the Arizona Society of CPA's. I ran a game show with them called "Are You Smarter than a 5th Grader – Estate Planning Edition." The response pads were smartphones for the whole audience, with an active leader board. Safe to say: I am not your typical attorney.

Why Now?

"Estate planning is morbid. Who wants to talk about their own demise?" That's a valid criticism. It is probably a major reason why people procrastinate creating an estate plan. Just as Robin Williams in *Dead Poets Society* stood on the desk to remind himself that we must constantly look at things in a different way, I put a different spin on estate planning. There's no getting around the fact that what we are preparing for is death and incapacity. Like it or not, we are mortal. But this doesn't have to be the focus.

Think about every asset you have. Now add the value of insurance policies. Do you have a number? If you could use those funds right now to best change the lives of the people you love and boost the causes you care about, what would you do with the money? That's the power of legacy.

And the younger you are when you start the estate planning process, the greater the likelihood is that the number will grow--even exponentially--as can the dreams of the difference you might make in the world.

Aren't All Estate Planning Documents Created Equal?

I have access to a tremendous legal network in WealthCounsel. This is a national group of estate planning attorneys who share expertise, training, knowledge, answer questions, and provide the most solid core set of legal documents in the industry. Then I customize each document for you, your family, your causes, your values, and your purposes.

Chapter 5: What's Your Story?

If you've ever owned a business, you've probably
spent many lunches and evenings networking.
You probably at least tried a BNI, speed
networking, and a Chamber of Commerce.
Suffice it to say, I network. A lot.

Just an aside—if you need to meet anyone, in just
about any profession in Phoenix—ask. I probably
know someone.

Perhaps the best early decision I made in the first
six weeks of my business was to follow my gut
after I received an email from Gelie Akhenblit. I
had never met her. I knew nothing about her. But
her email compelled me to buy a (very
inexpensive) passport to attend local Networking
Phoenix events. With that passport, I have
attended numerous events that are now core to
my business including the Phoenix Metro
Chamber of Commerce, Shakers & Stirrers, and
Networking REI. People from these groups have
formed other groups that are also red circled
dates on my calendar.

In January of 2019, I got to meet (and thank)
Gelie. This incredible woman has built a network
of 40,000 subscribers. She shared some tips for

building a network that I captured from pages of furiously scribbled notes. Some pieces I've heard echoes of in previous workshops (Larry Larson and David Hepburn come to mind). I'll put some of it in my own words, but I've got Gelie's permission to share.

1. Be Memorable – try conversation starters that throw people off the rehearsed script and start a genuine conversation with a possible new friend.

2. Be Me – use a personal conversation style in networking events and follow-ups, use pictures, and let people get to know the real person, not just the job title.

3. Be Intentional - pick events where your targeted audience will be, and attend at least five a month.

4. Develop Systems for Responding - make the response individual and do so in 48 hours. This may require sorting business cards by the type of relationship (clients, referral partners, resource people, and friends).

5. Be an Inviter - even if you can't attend – and occasionally host a meetup.

Number 1 is especially relevant. What's the first question that we usually ask someone we've never met?

What do you do?

I've never thought of that as an insensitive question. When you think about it, it is not a good opener. It closes off the conversation.

If the person says they drive in the Indy 500, you might tune in. But as soon as you realize they sell insurance or Melaleuca, listening ears turn off. This human person in front of you might have become a recurring referral source, an A-list client, or a close friend. By categorizing them in the "professions" box, all meaningful conversation is simply shut down.

Gelie encourages instead the much more engaging opener, "What's your story?" This question catches people off-guard. They have to actually think about how they engage. And you find out interesting tidbits that make them much more interesting.

So what's my story?

From middle school, I've always believed I would be an attorney, but it was not a direct path. I majored in my undergrad studies in Psychology and ended up taking a detour when I discovered that I wanted a career that would be compatible with family. I was married at 21 before I completed college.

When my daughter and sons were babies, I finished my masters in Counseling. When the kids were two and three, we moved to Florida where my husband had accepted a job in Finance with Walt Disney World.

In the spring of 2004, my sixth year as a school counselor, my undergrad alma mater sent out a newsletter advertising the new law school that was planned to open in the fall. They announced full scholarships to eligible candidates. I shared the article with my husband and he said: "You'd be an idiot not to apply." To which I responded, "But we'd have to move to Virginia." He agreed to the crazy plan, which had me starting law school with children in third and fourth grade.

Despite the challenges, I completed law school and passed the Florida Bar in 2007 intending to move to Florida and start a law practice. But God laughed.

Between 2007 and 2008, the economy had
tanked and my husband couldn't find a job that
would relocate us back to Florida. In summer
2008, we ended up in Houston, Texas with him at
General Electric. I had missed the window to take
the Texas Bar, so I thought I would foray back
into school counseling for "one year" until I could
take the bar exam. I loved working in Texas high
schools, especially when my children were at the
high school with me.

Then it was my son's turn. His true triple-threat
talents dragged us to Hollywood, where he
attended Orange County School of the Arts and
my career took a back seat to "momaging" his.
When he decided to go to college (after a gap
year of auditioning full time in L.A.), we moved
again to be near my family.

I found a wonderful job as the district behavioral
coach for a high-needs school district in
southeastern Washington. I helped campuses
develop their behavior plans, then taught
teachers, counselors, and paraeducators how to
direct and manage behavior, and coached them
when they had particularly challenging students.

When my husband's job brought us to Phoenix, I was at a loss. After 15 years in public education, it would be a $30,000 pay cut to remain in education in Arizona.

I had just enrolled in the first class of a Doctoral program in Education and was trying to determine what to do next when I attended my law school's ten-year reunion. Josh Dorcey grabbed me by the arm and said, "You need to be doing what I'm doing." I replied, "What are you doing?" He said, "Estate planning."

I looked at him with chagrin. "I'd have to take the bar exam in Arizona." "Yes, and when you do, you can spend a week with me [in Florida] to learn what I do."

It was a crazy idea. But as I examined estate planning, it was the same skill set. It is educating, counseling, coaching, and advising clients. So I sat for the Arizona Bar exam. (I may have been the only grandmother taking the exam.) Then I opened a law practice in Estate Planning after studying the content and spending some time observing Mr. Dorcey, Esq.

The name "Lifeguarding Legacies" partly came out of playing with my grandson. I look at him

and can't help but think that my job is to do
better for him—that's my legacy. And the
Lifeguarding piece comes from my near
obsession with the beach. I have to dig my feet
into the sand and tide at least twice a year. It also
allows me to talk about how I do "guard"
people's legacies from the things that life throws
at them, things like divorce, lawsuits, and family
strife.

It was a winding road, but that middle school girl
who thought she'd be a lawyer someday is now
living the dream.

Chapter 6: Role Call

There's a viral video of a substitute teacher who gets very upset as he conducts roll call, poorly pronouncing each one. If you haven't seen it, just put down this book and go to YouTube right now and type in "Substitute Teacher – Key & Peele" for a whole belly laugh.

However, we're not talking about that kind of roll call. We're talking about the roles that you need to know for a trust.

The Grantor

First, there's the Grantor. This is the one who is setting up the trust (and for our purposes here, we're going to say that's you). You are granting your possessions to the trust. Some lawyers will call this the Settlor or Trustor.

The Trustee

Next there is the Trustee. This is the person who retains control over the Trust. The terms of the trust dictate what the Trustee's power are, but often, they sell, give away, distribute, invest, account for, and manage the assets that are owned by the trust.

Ordinarily, you are the Trustee during your lifetime and you appoint the successor Trustees who will take over this job when you are incapacitated or pass away.

The Beneficiary

Third is the Beneficiary. This is the person who you created the trust to benefit. Most of the time, during your lifetime you are the Beneficiary, and after you pass, the family members or charities of your choice become the beneficiaries.

Interrelationships

There are some important relationships between these three primary roles. In a Revocable Living Trust, you usually serve in all three roles during your lifetime. However, it is important to remember that you have no real asset protection from your creditors, divorce, or lawsuits. This makes sense because during your lifetime, you still control the assets and benefit from them. Your revocable living trust is just a reflection of you, with a number of legal benefits that take effect when you become deceased.

Unless your trust allows self-dealing (most don't), your successor Trustee will owe a fiduciary duty to the Beneficiaries to manage the funds well. This means that the Trustee can't invest poorly, fail to keep records, or pay themselves more than industry pay to manage your trust. A trustee can be personally sued by a beneficiary for failing to conduct the job in a reasonable manner.

The Trust Protector

The Trust Protector is your genie in a bottle. He understands your wishes and works to make sure that your intentions are fulfilled. Not all trusts have a trust protector.

The trust protector is often the lawyer who drafted the document. The trust protector only gets involved if the trust is not doing what it was intended to do or a trustee isn't fulfilling his duties to the beneficiaries.

For example, let's say that a trust provided for the youngest of three children to remain in the family home for the child's lifetime. The attorney was with the client to formulate the trust while the client believed that this was a good plan.

Let's say the client has been deceased for 10 years. Now all three children are married. The youngest child doesn't want to live in the home anymore, but the trust really didn't make provision for selling the home. The Trust Protector can seek agreement from the trustee and beneficiaries to agree to sell the home. He can help the trustee to reasonably divide the proceeds in a way the client would have intended had he been here--without the beneficiaries having to go to court.

In reality, that's probably a bad example, because it would be poor drafting that would have left out a provision for the home to be sold. Nonetheless, it illustrates the role of the Trust Protector.

Chapter 7: Not One Size Fits All

Each Halloween in our neighborhood, we gather in a neighbor's driveway around a firepit. We greet hundreds of trick-or-treaters in a wide array of creative costumes. I confess I will always be drawn to the Disney classic princesses. And there is no tale as retold as that of Cinderella. The big take away—it was all about the way the shoe fit. (Maybe that's why it is one of my favorites!)

A good attorney can create an estate plan that fits just like that glass slipper. It will be customized just for you, to ensure that the legacy you want to leave is what your family inherits. Don't believe for a minute the fairy tale that a trust is only for the spoiled entitled rich kids that make headlines with their antics. The reality is that trusts are a foundational estate planning tool with a solid history for ensuring a person's wishes are carried out.

Better than a magic wand, the trust provides a means for protecting your property after your lifetime from divorce, lawsuits, creditors, and more.

Types of Trusts

- Revocable Living Trusts. As the name suggests, these trusts are revocable—meaning that during your lifetime you can change, remove assets, or cancel these trusts. They are also living (in Arizona for up to 500 years!), so they don't die. Whatever you put into these trusts avoids probate. Because they are so flexible and beneficial, they are the basis of many estate plans.

- Incentive Trusts. You can have control from beyond the grave! Trusts can be customized to share your family's values and make people engage in appropriate behaviors to earn what you leave behind.

- Beneficiary Controlled Trusts. I'll confess that I'm not a fan of these. Just as the name implies, the beneficiary controls the assets as the trustee. This eliminates some legal protections the beneficiary would have if an independent trustee were managing the assets.

- Domestic Asset Protection Trusts (DAPTs). These are not available yet in Arizona, but there is a team drafting legislation that might make these available in the next couple of years.

Right now, you can't shield yourself from your own creditors, lawsuits, or judgments by creating a trust. Other states have DAPTs, and our Arizona lawyers are watching these get tested before bringing them "to market." But I fully expect that there will be extra steps you must take to keep these legal protections in place, much like the paperwork you must keep in a business to keep yourself from personal liability.

- Offshore Trusts. For those who have extraordinarily high net worth and care about privacy and asset protection, it might be worth looking into an offshore trust. At this point, I do not offer these in my practice, but will bring in co-counsel who can help us with this advanced tax planning.

- Life Insurance Trusts. If you have a taxable estate, it might be worth considering an irrevocable life insurance trust (ILIT). The downside is that you cannot change or control this trust once it is setup. But it does have some terrific tax benefits. In 2020, this is only worth consideration if your assets as a married couple are over $23.16 million (or $11.58 million single). But that number might about cut in half in 2026. If you have an estate worth

5 million, let's plan a group chat with your financial advisor and your CPA.

- Testamentary Trusts. This isn't a real trust at all. Let's say a parent creates a will to establish guardianship for a minor child. But wants to ensure that if the parent dies while the child is still young, that the money is held in trust for the child's health, education, maintenance, and support. This language can be placed in a will, and the trust is created upon the parent's death. However, because it is still a will and not an existing trust, the will still goes through probate unless there is a good asset protection plan in place.

You don't need a fairy godmother to make sense of all of this, but you do need a good estate planning attorney to give you that perfect fit. One size does not fit all, but the right plan can turn your wishes into reality.

Chapter 8: The Faces and Phases of Estates

The Young Adult

You don't own anything other than maybe a car,
computer, gaming system, and some furniture.
You're not married. And you don't have kids.
Why in the world would you need an estate plan?
The value of your estate is under $75,000, so in
Arizona, your Personal Representative would just
file a small estate affidavit to avoid probate.
Everything would go to your parents. And that's
as it should be.

But wait. Think about your parents for a minute.
What would happen to them if you were in an
accident? You are alive, but spend some time in
the hospital unconscious. It happens to someone
every single day.

Your parents have no legal right to find out your
medical status (even if you are still on their
insurance!). They have no right to make your
medical decisions. They have no responsibility to
secure insurance or help with the medical bills.
You are a ward of the state--just like a foster
child. The state decides what care you will
receive.

If your parents want to fight for the right to be your advocate, they would need to hire a lawyer and seek legal guardianship. This is expensive and unnecessary.

The parents who helped you learn to ride a bike, sat with you to you recite your spelling words, and bought you your first iPhone would welcome a hand from you here. My guess is that most parents would happily pay the legal fees for the peace of mind of having your medical documents and powers of attorney in place.

Parents of young adults—before you you're your kids to college, you can help them and preserve your ability to step in during an emergency. Get a financial power of attorney, a healthcare power of attorney, a living will (also known as an advance directive), and a HIPAA waiver in place so that you can help your child take the next step in her transition to responsible adulthood.

The Fur Baby's Parent

Very often before there are children, there are pets. Sometimes, the pets remain the children and sometimes the pets welcome the children.

Arizona law is very accommodating to the parents of fur babies. In both wills and trusts there are specialty provisions that allow us to determine who will care for your pet and will allow us to set aside money, terms, and conditions for that care.

I had one case where the retired veteran client had beloved, well-trained service dogs. They went everywhere he went. No one would ever question his loyalty to the dogs. He wanted the dogs buried in caskets and wanted them to live out their natural lives in his home with a pet caretaker.

Such an arrangement would delay family members from taking their full inheritance, but would likely stand in such a case because he had a recognized pattern of his pets being such a central part of his life.

The New Parent

You still may not have many assets, but you have the biggest gift and responsibility in the world. New eyes watch and depend on your every move. You need a will. You need a document that assigns guardianship so that if something happens to you, you determine who would best love and protect your child.

In the absence of a will, the child temporarily becomes a ward of the state and hearings commence on who is best suited to care for your child. The legal fees can be overwhelming to your small estate. Add to that the trauma of being stuck in the middle of battling relatives if family begins to fight over the care of the child.

It is possible that you've already worked hard to provide the stability of home ownership for your child. If the deed reads "right of survivorship" with your spouse or co-parent, then unless the two of you pass simultaneously, the surviving spouse will own the home without probate. If you are a single parent with a home, it is time to consider your options.

In Arizona, we have the option of Beneficiary deeds, which are an affordable way to modify your deed so that when you die, the house passes to the person listed on the deed and avoids probate. Most states do not have such an option.

The other option is to create a revocable living trust. You can deed the house to the trust. You still retain full control. You can sell the home, take equity out of the home, and remodel the home. The trust will live on past you to ensure that the home passes to the family members of your choice under the terms you decide.

The Partner or Fiancée

You may be deeply in love, but you're not in a legally recognized relationship. In order for a doctor to talk to your significant other, you need paperwork that recognizes the person in a legal way. You'll need the same legal powers of attorney and medical documents as a young adult.

If you've accumulated some wealth, you will likely want to create a will or a trust to leave your belongings to your partner.

You should also consider how real estate should be held to ensure that your property passes to your partner. If you want to own the home yourself, but want your partner to inherit it, you could select a Beneficiary Deed. If you want to share all the rights to the property now and have the survivor inherit the property, you could have the property deeded with joint right of survivorship. Or you may want a trust to own the property so that you can design a more complex distribution plan that includes this real estate as well as your other belongings.

The Divorcee

You and your spouse built your lives together. You may have even created a will or trust together. You were each other's beneficiaries on all your retirement accounts and life insurance policies. But happily ever after didn't last.

It's time to rebuild, redefine, and refocus.

First and foremost: change your beneficiaries. My son-in law's grandmother was recently engaged to be married to a man who had been divorced. He passed suddenly with heart issues. And his ex got everything.

Next: examine your divorce decree. You've hopefully already consulted a lawyer before the divorce settlement so the final decree should be fair. Now it is time to legally retitle property in your name. If you choose to have the deed in your solo name, the property will go through probate. Consider a beneficiary deed or put the property into a trust.

Finally: select a will or trust package that suits your predicted needs in your new life.

The Blended Family

Whether it's Cheaper by the Dozen, the Brady Bunch, or Yours, Mine & Ours, we know that life gets complicated when two families merge. There's no getting around it: you need a more complex plan.

Your custody arrangements may be somewhat decided by your divorce decrees, but you don't want what you are building in your new marriage to end up with your ex. And what you built with your ex you may still want for your children.

There are a number of designs that can meet these unique needs. We need to make sure we provide for the surviving spouse and both sets of prior families.

It may make sense to make the trust irrevocable when the first spouse dies so that the arrangements for distributions to children can't be changed in favor of one set of siblings.

It may make sense to create a marital trust and two separate trusts for the children.

Or it might make sense to have everything except the interest from investments, the primary checking, and the family home to go to the children 50% to hers, 50% to his. There is no one-size-fits-all in these discussions. But they are critical discussions.

The Grandparent

Of all the groups here, these are my people. Something happens when you hold a grandchild for the first time. Just like the grinch whose heart grew three sizes that day, your capacity to love just multiples when you encounter your third generation.

And for many of us whose kids maybe didn't follow the straightest of paths, we know the hard roads that lie ahead for our kids and how that will affect the tiny fingers that now grasp our own babies' hands.

We are faced with a new reality that our help is needed, emotionally and financially.

As grandparents face our mortality in estate planning, we have a bit of a different leaning. We ask--if I don't outlive my money, what difference can I make for the third generation?

Personally, upon my untimely demise, my independent Trustee (my brother-in-law) will write a check marked yes to everything my grandchildren might want to do to enhance their lives and education.

Summer camp – Yes
Traveling baseball team – Yes
Horseback riding lessons – Yes
Violin – Yes
Ballet - Yes
Golf - Yes
Missions trip - Yes
Hula hoop on skateboards – Probably
Skydiving – Well, maybe not that

I expect that my kids will provide housing, food, and access to education. I get to provide all those extras that enrich the lives of my grandchildren.

And of course, I'll help with college or postsecondary training, a first home, and a few other success measures.

To do these kinds of specialty distributions, only a trust will do. It requires a willing, involved, unbiased, and financially responsible trustee.

The Business Owner

As a business owner, asset protection must be a primary concern. You should structure your business to have holdings in different entities that maximize your tax savings and minimize your risk. For example, you may own real estate rentals in LLCs, so that if someone were to slip and fall, they can only sue that one LLC and not you or your overall business. This area can become extraordinarily complex.

In the simplest of terms, you want to have as many of the things you own out of your name as possible. In your case, I would absolutely recommend a revocable living trust for your family assets, and then an arrangement between the businesses and the trust to ensure that only the value of the business passes to your children, but they retain no liability or management responsibility. Essentially, the trust is made a shareholder.

If you do not have a good CPA or business entities strategist, please allow me to introduce you. This should be part of the foundation upon which we build your estate plan.

You should also have discussions with a business broker to develop a succession plan for selling the business when you are ready to retire and an emergency exit plan if something were to happen to you.

If you not a solopreneur, but have a business partner who would struggle if something were to happen to you, I'd also recommend having the conversation with your insurance broker or financial planner about Key Person Insurance. I don't sell insurance, but Key Person Insurance provides income to the business to continue in your absence.

There are numerous additional asset protection strategies you should consider. These were intended as just a few to get you started down the right path.

Legacy Builders

Not every retiree has a third generation. Several of my clients have been older single adults. They have the unique opportunity to think about the difference they might make in the world by

selecting meaningful charities or setting up a
Foundation.

One such client who had never married or had
children had a large extended family. Her family
was financially secure (many were truly wealthy).
They didn't need her money.

In her case, we sat down and talked about each
family member. After much discussion, we were
able to find a charitable organization or cause for
each family member, and gave a percentage of
her estate to each. It was truly a beautiful thing
to look at how her life's work will touch so many
lives and leave an enduring tribute to her family
members.

Chapter 9: What's the Process?

Let Your GPS Guide You

I'll confess right now: I am one of the lucky ones. This spring, my husband and I will celebrate 28 years of marriage and I still feel like celebrating. We had an unseasonably beautiful morning wedding on March 21, 1992. In the evening, we started our three plus hour drive to Seattle. We would spend one night there then catch the early morning ferry to honeymoon in Victoria, British Columbia.

We easily made it to Seattle. That city--with all its one-way streets and confusing signs--had us running in circles for over two hours. And just like the stereotype, my husband simply refused to ask for directions. I was tired, cranky, and temporarily questioning my life choices.

We learned to avoid road trips in those early years. It just wasn't worth the headache.

Our first Garmin GPS navigation system was a game-changer. It kept me from pestering my husband to stop for help on our adventures. Knowing our destination and letting a machine give us the play-by-play reduced my nagging to the more urgent sudden stops and following too closely. And now with phone apps like Waze, we can even get around traffic and other road obstacles. Yes, GPS may have saved our marriage.

Knowing your destination is important, but we also need a plan to get there. I wonder if people don't feel the same about estate planning. They have a general idea of how they want things to go, but figure since they haven't worked out the details, they can't start the trip. Instead, let me serve as your GPS, your Guide for Process Solutions.

If you come in for a free consultation, I will ask you the questions that will direct each decision as we navigate the legal planning process together. You will be amazed at how creative the process really is and how good it feels to check this daunting task off the list. It's like that feeling when you arrive at the beach on the perfect day after months of planning the getaway trip. Except, you won't be sunburned afterward.

Your Backstory Matters

A friend posted an uncredited story on Facebook last year.

Last Wednesday a passenger in a taxi heading for Midway airport, leaned over to ask the driver a question and gently tapped him on the shoulder to get his attention.

The driver screamed, lost control of the cab, nearly hit a bus, drove up over the curb, and stopped just inches from a large plate window.

For a few moments everything was silent in the cab. Then, the shaking driver said, "Are you OK? I'm so sorry, but you scared the daylights out of me."

The badly shaken passenger apologized to the driver and said, "I didn't realize that a mere tap on the shoulder would startle someone so badly."

The driver replied, "No, no, I'm the one who is sorry, it's entirely my fault. Today is my very first day driving a cab. I've been driving a Hearse for 25 years."

If the passenger knew the backstory, she would never have tapped the driver on the shoulder. She'd have taken another cab. Or kept chit-chat

steady throughout the ride. Or just remained
completely silent.

Backstories matter. Knowing that you want to
give your desk to your nephew is easy enough to
include in a will or trust. Knowing that your
nephew is being recognized because he helped
take your child to kindergarten every day is even
better. And knowing that your grandfather
carved that desk from the tree under which he
proposed to your grandmother helps complete
the backstory. Stories behind your heirlooms
might convince that now minimalist nephew not
to dump the desk at Goodwill.

These stories can also communicate with family
how you treasure and appreciate them.

It is also helpful to capture your family values. Is
travel a big deal? What about your religious
practice? Your civic involvement? Certain
charities you support? Your pets? Sports and
recreation? What drives you? What inspires
you? Someone may have to make decisions for
you if you reach a place of incapacity or when
you pass and that person should have a clear
picture of the things that matter most so that
they can fulfill your wishes with clarity and
purpose.

Share your backstories. They may mean more than you'd believe. They may be Chicken Soup for your Family's Soul.

Intake Decisions

Do you suffer from analysis paralysis? Do decisions stress you out? The part of the process that people sometimes find overwhelming are the many decisions that must be made. This is yet another stumbling block that can cause people to procrastinate on their estate plans. Yet with your GPS, you can make these decisions in smaller turn-by-turn fashion.

Most of the decisions involve naming someone to serve in a role. Sometimes, with just a description of the role a person's face comes to mind without a moment's hesitation. Sometimes, there is no one who can fill that role. Sometimes, there are several people who would all fill the role and it is a matter of choosing the right one to serve first.

The Guardian for Minor Children

Deciding who would become the guardian for your child upon your death is by far the most important decision you will make. The very thought of someone else becoming the parent of your child is almost unimaginable.

If you are married and the children are shared, your spouse will, of course, be the guardian.

If you are previously divorced and the divorce decree allowed for shared custody, your ex will be the guardian with likely visitation allowed for your spouse.

In the other instances, this decision is left up to you (or you and your spouse). You are a far better judge than any court when it comes to your child. If you fail to make this decision, the court will. Interested family members and friends would petition the court to become guardian and a very costly legal battle may ensue. In the interim, the child becomes a ward of the state and may even be placed in foster care.

Both wills and trusts offer provisions for the important decision of guardianship. I recommend to clients that the key questions to ask are:
- Who loves my child most?
- Who would be most likely to make the same decisions I would make?

- With whom would my child want to live?
- Who would create a new home that poses the least disruption to my child's life?
- Who would best be able to deal with the emotional challenges of my child losing me?

You'll notice that I didn't mention money or the ability to provide for the child. Even if you have a very small estate, if you are considering a will or trust, you should also consider life insurance as part of this plan. At least term life insurance. For $30 or less a month you can purchase $500,000 in term life insurance to help take care of your child. I don't sell insurance. I never plan to do so. But it seems such a basic protection to have in place to ensure that your child has a livelihood if something were to happen to you.

Now let's talk about money management. If the person who would best fit the description of guardian is terrible with money, maybe they should not be the one to collect the life insurance proceeds. Sometimes it makes sense to distribute money to separate hands from the hands providing the caregiving.

As a parent of a minor child with a very small estate, consider a testamentary trust. This is just a will, but it contains provisions that upon your death, your assets will be placed in a trust for the care of your minor children. Consider appointing an independent trustee to manage the money who is not the guardian for your children. As with every will package, it is important to protect assets in a way that can avoid probate.

If you are a parent of a minor child with a growing estate, you should consider a revocable living trust with an independent trustee who is not the guardian of your children. While the trust costs more than a will up front, it may cost less to manage later. In the trust, we can design a distribution pattern that is customized to each age and stage of your child's development.

The Personal Representative

The Personal Representative is Arizona's term for the Executor. This is the person who will take care of the probate (or other filings) of your estate, complete the estate sale, and distribute items under your will. Here's what you should look for:
- Reasonable decision-maker
- Trustworthy
- Unbiased toward your family members
- A natural peacemaker

- Can do a relatively simple accounting spreadsheet if needed to account to family members
- Will honor your wishes

Unless there is a dispute, courts try to have as little supervision as possible over the personal representative.

The Trustee

The Trustee is the person who controls your Trust assets and handles all issues and distributions under your trust. There is no court involvement unless someone files a lawsuit.

You should pick someone who meets all the criteria for a Personal Representative, but also has the Midas touch with money management. I have a brother-in-law who can rub two nickels together and make a ten-dollar bill. He is an excellent investor, a savvy businessman, and a practical thinker. He will make an excellent Trustee. The Trustee is generally expected to keep assets invested well and to provide an annual report to the beneficiaries. Money management is truly critical.

In the next chapter we'll cover why your child should not be your Trustee.

If you come from a family that doesn't handle money well, don't despair. There are professional fiduciaries who can be appointed to handle your financial affairs when you can't. Just like any other professional, some are better than others and some are more ethical in their billing practices. I would suggest those that take 1-2% of the estate each year over those who charge by each task they perform or each check they write. It is reasonable to expect that interest on your estate's investments should outperform the 1-2% costs that a fiduciary would charge.

The General Durable Power of Attorney

The General Durable Power of Attorney (DPOA) is the document that appoints the person who will pay your bills and manage your money if you are incapacitated. The person you designate as DPOA will often be called your Agent. The agent is a fiduciary, which means she has the legal obligation to act in your interest, not her own interest.

Incapacity is a legal term that basically means "unable to make your own decisions." In these documents, incapacity happens when two or more doctors responsible for your care agree by signed affidavits that you are incapable of caring for your personal safety or unable to handle daily living tasks such as feeding, dressing, securing adequate shelter, taking necessary medications, or handling your financial affairs.

It is important to note that the Agent is not responsible for actually helping you feed, dress, or take medications. The Agent is only responsible for acting in your shoes on your financial matters.

You can limit what kinds of matters you will allow your Agent to handle. Do you want them to continue to give gifts on your behalf when you can't? Should they be able to secure life insurance policies for your life? Should they be able to sell property? Run your business?

In most cases, the Trustee of your trust will also serve as your Agent for incapacity under the DPOA.

One important side note: banks can be creatures of policy. Sometimes their policies are a pain in the backside. If your Agent waits until you are incapacitated to reveal the DPOA forms, some banks will balk and create a paper nightmare to gain access to funds. Other banks are terrific. (You can ask me to name names.) It is better to share your forms with your bank while you are healthy and ensure that these are acceptable before the need arises. Some banks even have their own forms that they will want you to sign.

Your Healthcare Power of Attorney (HCPOA) is the person who is responsible for your medical decisions when you can no longer make them. The standard for incapacity is the same as it is for the DPOA. The HCPOA should be:
- Caring and compassionate
- A natural nurse
- Practical
- Able to balance family's needs against the cost of continued care
- Able to make difficult decisions under pressure
- Honor the way you would make decisions

A companion document to the HCPOA is a Living Will (also referred to as an Advance Directive). The Living Will makes some of the end of life decisions that you do not want to burden a family member with making.

HIPAA Authorized Recipients

Every year when you visit your doctor's office, you have to fill out a form. You list the family members names with whom the office may share your medical information. This is required by the Federal Health Insurance Portability and Accountability Act of 1996 (updated significantly in 2009). It makes sense to list your spouse and maybe one other on these doctor's office forms. The likelihood that they would have an issue arise where you are incapacitated and they need to be involved at the doctor's office is small.

However, you probably don't have a general HIPAA waiver on file with the hospital. Unless you are a frequent patient, you don't need one to be kept there. But you should have a more generic HIPAA waiver that is stored where family members can retrieve it in an emergency situation. My clients have access to a secure electronic portal where their scanned signed documents may be retrieved and sent at a moment's notice from any device.

There are different philosophies about who should be listed on a HIPAA waiver to be used in emergency situations when you can't sign your own form on admittance.

My personal opinion is that you should list any close friend or family member who would be likely to show up in a waiting room. Anyone with whom you would want a doctor to be able to share your status.

Remember, this form will only be used if you are in a situation where you can't fill out a standard HIPAA form at check-in.

One other important note here. All other estate planning documents are evergreen: they live until they are revoked by a more current document. But HIPAA waivers only last for two years. My clients get an email reminder a few weeks before their HIPAA waivers expire to get these forms updated.

People Data

We'll need the following general information for you and your spouse prior to drafting documents:
- Legal name
- Date of Birth
- Social Security Number (for HIPAA Waiver)
- US Citizen?
- Addresses for all owned properties
- Best Email and Phone
- Date of Marriage

For children, people listed to fill the many roles described in this chapter, and other beneficiaries, we need only their legal names, dates of birth, and how they are related.

It is also helpful to have the contact information for your personal attorney, accountant, financial advisor, and life insurance agent.

Intake Decisions

The hardest decisions in estate plans are identifying the people to fill all the roles above. Once you have faces and names, it is easier to decide what powers you might give or withhold from them based on your relationship with them.

However, there are a slew of other smaller decisions to make, and this is not intended to be a comprehensive list, but is certainly good preparation for an intake appointment:
- What personal possessions do you want to specifically gift to a particular person or charity?
- Are you disinheriting someone?
- Are you providing for a child with disabilities?
- Are you concerned about the stability of a child's current marriage?

- Are you receiving any social security, disability, or governmental benefits?
- Are you divorced? (If so, we'll need a copy of the property settlement order.)
- Do you have a previous will or trust? (It is a good idea to bring this with you.)
- Do you plan to support charities?
- Are you expecting an inheritance from another? Or are you the beneficiary of someone's trust?
- What types of assets do you have (in some detail for trusts, less detail for wills)?
- Does someone owe you money?
- Any known or possible lawsuits?
- Are you an organ donor? Transplantation or research?
- Cremation or burial? And have you already made arrangements?
- Do you want your HCPOA to take whatever steps are necessary to keep you in a personal residence rather than a nursing home?
- Do you trust your HCPOA enough to authorize them to seek voluntary psychiatric or drug abuse treatment if you need it?

- Does your trustee need to balance your needs with those of your beneficiaries, or is it okay if your needs significantly deplete your estate?
- Do you want to give equal amounts to grandchildren? Or do you want the equal amount to be divided among your children and their children divide the parents' share?
- Do you want one-lump sum distributions? Distributions upon certain birthdays? More specific distributions?
- Do you wish to provide for fur babies?
- Any special considerations for your family home?

As you can see, there is much to think about. But don't panic, the GPS will get you there step-by-step and turn-by-turn.

I'm sure you can see how difficult it would be to make all these considerations fit on a fill-in-the-blank Google form.

Chapter 10: Why You Shouldn't Trust Your Kids

Kids don't have to be taught to be sneaky. Before he was two, my grandson would look to see if we were watching before he'd touch the Christmas tree ornaments. He knew better.

We learn in time to set limits and grow trust in our kids. My favorite teen strategy was "trust, but verify." Occasionally and unpredictably verify that kids are where and with whom they said they would be.

But there are some things with which you should never trust your kids. The big one is actually your trust.

A common estate planning mistake, in my opinion, is to have your child be the trustee of your trust. Sure, they are the ones who are likely to organize the estate sale. They are the ones who will have to run errands and request paperwork. But if you are planning to have ongoing gifts to your children (which to me is the biggest reason to have a trust), your son or daughter should not be the one in control.

Here's why. Let's say you have a very reliable daughter. She gets into a fender bender. Then you end up with a money grubber who decides to fund her own retirement on the bad back she's always had but now blames your daughter for aggravating. If your daughter is the trustee, any funds that would disperse to her are now attachable in the lawsuit.

If you have an independent trustee who has some discretion over the gifts, the trustee can pay your daughter's bills directly and ensure she has what she needs. Only what is actually deposited to an account would be attachable. If done right, nothing is attachable. Money grubbing fender lady has to find another victim.

Here's another reason why you shouldn't trust your child as trustee. Imagine your son is going through a nasty divorce. Any funds that have been comingled into accounts are going to be split with his ex. And any ongoing scheduled payments or money over which he has discretion are possible considerations for alimony. But an independent trustee with discretion can similarly withhold these payments and keep this money out of reach.

Who should you trust as your trustee? There are two primary qualifying questions. 1) Who is someone so knowledgeable and proficient with money that they could host Dave Ramsey's radio show? And 2) Who can be unbiased toward the beneficiaries you listed in your trust?

If you have someone in mind, fantastic! If not, it may be worth the 1-2% of your estate each year to protect your kids with a professional trustee.

Yet, there are those who can't be trusted. So be careful of those who charge by the hour or by the task. Some have been known to wipe out estates with their excessive involvement and costs. They're a little like my grandson, trying to get their hands on shiny objects.

You've worked hard to build your estate plan: make sure you leave it in capable and trusted hands. And just don't trust your kids: protect them from their own lives by keeping them out of control of your trust.

Chapter 11: The Dangers of the Deep: 5 biggest mistakes in estate planning

I've mentioned before, I'm nearly obsessed with beaches. Sandy shores, gently swaying palm trees, and turquoise waters beckon me. Vacations for me must have palm trees or theme parks (and preferably both)! I sleep refreshed when I can breathe in the salty ocean air and feel most alive when my feet are bare in the sand.

Yet I find I don't stray far from shore. I still have very real fears about the teeth and perils that lie beneath the surface of the water.

It was no surprise that I found metaphors to teach estate planning mistakes based on the dangers of the deep.

The Ruthless Rays of Probate

Have you ever watched rays in the wild (or in one of those petting tanks at an aquarium)? I find myself completely mesmerized watching them gently dance through the water. They seem harmless.

Steve Irwin (the Australian "Crocodile Hunter)
proved that even the experienced nature lover
could feel the sting of death from these elegant
creatures.

Frank's big mistake was not quite so perilous.
But it still stung his family. Frank made the first
of our 5 top estate planning mistakes. He
believed his will was all he needed. He didn't
consult with a lawyer to ensure that his asset
protection plan would work.

He owned a home with more than $100k of
equity that was titled only to him. The house
triggered a probate on his death. It should have
been deeded to a family member by a Beneficiary
Deed or placed in a trust.

Now there's a 4-month window when creditors
get to swim around and make claims against
Frank's estate.

In the meantime, Frank's estate is locked up
tighter than a tackle box, other than a few
allowances and exclusions.

Probate for Frank's will is likely to cost his estate
at least $3-6 thousand, but if there is a contest, it
can cost tens of thousands (or more!). And it is a

hassle and a burden on the family members still grieving his loss.

A will is just a letter to the probate court that tells them how you want your assets distributed. By itself a will cannot avoid probate. A will plus asset planning might have been enough. The other option is a revocable living trust.

Let's talk about that trust.

First it's revocable, meaning that during your lifetime you can change it, move assets around, or rewrite the whole thing.

Second, it's living, meaning that it doesn't die. Because it doesn't die, it doesn't go to probate. In fact, it can live on for up to 500 years in Arizona or until all its purposes are fulfilled.

Not to be Frank, make sure you develop a good asset plan along with your will, or choose a revocable living trust. Don't make the mistake of believing that a will will do.

The Jolting Jellyfish of Incapacity

I've never been scuba diving. One time in Cabo, I
went through the short training, donned the
wetsuit, practiced the breathing, and was ready
to dive off the side of the boat. But the water
was full of jellyfish. The instructor jumped in and
was attacked with unpleasant electrical impulses.
Just talking about it, I have sympathy pains.

When people think about estate planning, they
usually think about planning for their death, but
that's big mistake #2. It is just as important to set
a plan in place for incapacity.

Now you might be thinking that I'm talking about
dementia. If that's where your mind is going, you
are likely to tune me out thinking that you can
procrastinate.

But let's say you are in a serious car accident and
the ambulance takes you to the hospital in a
coma. It happens every day.

If it happened to you, do you have documents in
place that allow those you care about to talk to
the doctors on your behalf? Someone assigned
to make the medical decisions? Someone
assigned to take care of the finances?

If you are over 18, you need key documents in place. Otherwise, a family member may have the high legal fees and loss of critical time seek legal guardianship through the court system.

Oh, that stings! And it is often sudden and unpredictable. But you can choose jolt-free waters. Will and trust plans include the supporting documents of healthcare power of attorney, financial power of attorney, a living will, and a HIPAA waiver.

The War-Waging Eels of Family Strife

I found a National Geographic video on YouTube that shows two Moray Eels spinning around as they fight to the death. It is one of those "I don't want to watch, but can't take my eyes off it" videos.

My mind went to a couple of teenage girls fighting over a boy (here hold my earrings). These vicious creatures were seeking to cause the deepest harm they possibly could.

That is mistake #3 in estate planning: believing that the kids will get along after you die.

There is an old joke in the legal world. Criminal law is bad people on their best behavior. Family law is good people on their worst behavior. And estate law is just family law with money.

I've seen it. Families that seemed perfect amicable. Thanksgivings and Christmases shared without a hitch. Then, mom passes.

There is always one object that at least two people want. Badly. One was promised it. The other might already have it in their possession. Then the fights get ugly.

We like to think that we aren't tied to possessions. Yet the sentimental pull of some objects is stronger than we think.

One lawyer even talked about how a family soaked up a majority of the money in a large estate over a $3 vacation knick-knack that had sentimental value to five children.

The only right way to limit these disputes is with pre-planning. Talk to your family members now. Learn what objects carry strong emotional value. It is much easier to mediate these disputes with mom involved than when she's gone.

Make a plan to distribute your assets to your family members that will limit the fighting and let you leave this world with your soul and your family at peace.

A Pirates Curse

Johnny Depp is arguably the best actor of all time. There was a popular meme that pictured him in his many roles: "They said I could be anything I want when I grew up. So I did." He's played everything from a weird kid with scissors on his hand to an Indian to Willy Wonka. Perhaps his best-beloved character is Captain Jack Sparrow in the Pirates of the Caribbean series.

Jack made pirates likeable.

At the end of the first movie, *The Curse of the Black Pearl*, there's a scene where he and a cursed group of skeletal pirates find a heap of buried treasure. The coins were cursed if they were removed from the chest.

A large treasure is often a curse in real life.

We all know the stories of millionaire lottery winners. They are most often more broke two years after they bought the ticket than they were beforehand. Most people do not handle great wealth that is suddenly bestowed. It takes years of training and positive habits to manage money well. And yet, most of us will leave an inheritance as one lump sum, even if just the value of our home.

This is rarely leaving a legacy. It will most often be used and spent within two years—as if cursed. Lump sum distributions are big estate planning mistake #4.

If you have large investments like 401ks, IRAs, large bank accounts, or real estate, think about how these might be divided and spread over time.

In my case, I follow the Warren Buffett philosophy: "You should leave your children enough so they can do anything, but not enough so they can do nothing." I want my kids to have to work for their living. But when I'm gone, I want their lives to be enriched by what I gave them.

My trust is set to give an adjusted amount based on the IRS gift tax exclusion. This isn't for tax reasons (inheritances in Arizona aren't taxed unless your married estate is over $22 million), but it is a nice number of $15,000 now and will continue to adjust for inflation. This is $1,250 per month. That's below the poverty line by a fair bit.

It is enough to buy a decent car every few years. Enough for a kitchen remodel. Enough for a few nice family vacations. Enough to enhance without substantially changing their lives.

I'll confess—there has been a complication in this arena. The SECURE Act of 2019 requires that inherited 401ks and IRAs be fully distributed within ten years so that the government gets its capital gains tax money. (There is a delay if the beneficiary is under age 18.) We used to be able to stretch that out through a whole lifetime.

This is one area where it can be helpful to meet with your estate planning attorney, your financial advisor, and your CPA. We can team together to make sure that your plan distributes the IRA and 401k money first, before bank accounts and proceeds from home sales, so that your children can experience the benefit of your legacy throughout their lifetime. So that your children never experience the pirates curse.

My husband believes Google is the evil empire. He is a bit of a conspiracy theorist, and sometimes he doesn't seem that far off. I won an Amazon Alexa device as a door prize, and he won't let me plug it in because he doesn't want to add more ways that our conversations might be listened to. Even so, I can't tell you how many times we've had a private conversation about buying something, then an ad appears on the screen in Google or in my Facebook feed for that very item. It's creepy.

Nevertheless, I think Google is ah-maze-ing. You can ask just about any question and get an instant (and usually right) answer. I am old enough to remember trying to use an old set of Encyclopedia Britannica's to find answers to questions my parents couldn't answer. Now I hit a button and Google comes to the rescue.

It makes perfect sense to Google a will form and fill in the blanks and sign it. And legally, it might hold up. Emphasis on MIGHT.

How old is that form? Does it really meet the needs of your family? Is it specific to the rules in your state? Does it take into account current law? Who wrote it? Were they good at what they did?

I could probably create a will form that would serve its basic purpose. But even with legal training, I wouldn't do that. I subscribe to WealthCounsel, which is recognized in the estate planning industry as the "Cadillac" of estate planning education, community, and core documents. They work tirelessly to ensure that state-specific documents are up to date. It is an investment that I think is very worthwhile in my business—and I never worry that my clients are getting less than the best.

As the Legacy Lifeguard, I work to ensure that my clients are protected from the dangers of the deep. Don't make estate planning mistake #5 and swim with no lifeguard on duty. You would be swimming at your own risk.

Chapter 12: More Than You Want to Know About Probate

What is Probate?

Probate is the legal way the state ensures that property passes to the rightful owners. The process has its roots way back in medieval England. If the Lord of a Castle died, those in power didn't want the peasant squatters claiming ownership.

In our much less distant history, the neighborly judge in many towns would review the will to make sure the property was assigned correctly and that anyone who was owed money would receive what they were entitled to receive. This is still the very useful and valid purpose of probate.

Why Do I Always Hear Horror Stories About Probate?

Like so many other problems: the answer is time and money.

We are actually very fortunate to live in Arizona. Not only for the weather, but our probate isn't too bad. In our sister snowbird state of Florida, probate commonly drag out for 18 months, with sky high legal fees.

In Arizona, creditors have four months from the time they receive notice to stake a claim in the estate. If there is no family dispute, then after the four-month period, everyone gets what they should (minus court and legal fees of course).

Without a will, the state intestate succession laws come into play. These laws treat all families the same. First to spouse and kids, then to parents, then siblings, and so on through a whole family tree. Most non-contested estates are settled in six months.

The problem is that until probate is done, the estate is basically locked up. You can't buy or sell property or spend money except what the state allows. Perhaps that's for the best, because people don't make the best financial and life decisions when they are grieving.

What Does the State Allow?

There is a state homestead allowance of $18,000 and a family allowance of $12,000 designed for the use of surviving spouses and children.

Creditors can't get at this $30,000 cash that families can draw from their assets to live on.

The family can also own $7,000 in cars, furniture, appliances, and personal effects that creditors can't touch.

That is probably sufficient for most families to get through the four-month period.

The families still at risk are those whose
- Family budget exceeds $7,500 a month
- Those who have more stuff, but have high debt that risk repossession
- Those without a will
- Those with a contestable will

What Kinds of Assets Does the Court Look at in Probate?

Simply put, if an item is "solely" owned by the deceased person, it counts as a probate asset. Jewelry, furniture, automobiles, solo bank accounts, and real estate titled solely in the deceased person's name are the main assets that creditors can attack before the family inherits.

That means that anything with two names on it can avoid probate. A shared checking account avoids probate. A house titled with right of survivorship avoids probate (unless both owners pass). Retirement accounts like IRAs and 401ks have beneficiaries assigned to pass without probate.

Does a Will Avoid Probate?

This is a common misperception. A will does not avoid probate. A will is like a letter to the court. It tells the court what you intend to do with your belongings after the creditors are paid.

Are There Different Types of Probate?

Yes. In Arizona there are three types of probate: informal, formal, and supervised. And there's a shortcut for small estates.

Affidavit for Small Estates

A small estate affidavit can be downloaded from the Arizona Department Health Services website. It is completed, a death certificate is attached, and voila—present these to claim items at banks and other asset holders with no probate. You attest on this form that the deceased person had less than $100k in real estate equity and less than

$75k as the sum total of all personal property titled in his name. Remember, this $75k is only items that don't already have a way to go to you around probate. The $75k doesn't include IRAs with beneficiary statements, PODs/TODs at banks, cars with beneficiary forms, life insurance, etc. The $75k does include household furnishings, jewelry, bank accounts in just the deceased person's name, items in safe deposit boxes, etc.

Simplified Probate

In its simplest terms, a simplified or summary probate is only for the small estates where the assets barely cover final expenses and leave only a small amount left over to support the spouse and children of the person who died. There are still some assets that are excluded (IRAs, life insurance, etc.).

Informal Probate

Most estates in Arizona will go through Informal Probate. This requires very little court supervision because there is no one filing a lawsuit for a dispute and family members have agreed to who should serve as the Personal Representative. Families can waive other

Personal Representative responsibilities as well (inventory of property and securing bond). The Personal Representative has to be pretty savvy to understand the training and documents without legal assistance. With legal assistance, this informal probate will cost the estate between $3-6k.

Formal Probate

This is the stuff of movies and nightmares. This is where the court steps in to solve all legal and family squabbles. Each disputing party will pay hourly legal fees that quickly chip away at the value of the estate. This can drag on for many months and sometimes years and can cost tens of thousands or more.

This is why estate planning is so important.

Don't Forget the Alternative

There is an easy solution to protect your assets from probate, your children's creditors, exes, and lawsuits. It is called a revocable living trust. It is revocable because you can change it during your lifetime. It is living because it never dies—that is how it avoids probate. Anything you own that would end up in probate should be owned by

your trust and not by you. A trust also allows
tremendous flexibility in controlling how assets
are distributed. It can be on a timeline, through a
set of values that must be met, or given outright.
Your trust, your way.

Chapter 13: Bad, Better, Best, and Worst Asset Protection Strategies

It is my hope that by this point in the book you are convinced that an estate plan absolutely involves asset protection strategies. You will hear "practical" advice from people on how you can avoid lawyers and create do-it-yourself asset remedies. Let's walk through a few of these strategies.

BAD: Include Child on Deed of Your Home

Real estate has to go through probate when the deceased person owned the property alone and had more than $100k in equity. It makes perfect sense then that no property should be owned in just one name.

If a parent's goal is to pass the property to an adult child, it would be logical to put his name on the deed of the home for a quick and easy transfer.

Yet here's another place you should never trust your kids.

If you have a falling out with your son, he can sell or sublet his half interest in your home to the tenant from the pit of Hades. (Watch the Michael Keaton thriller *Pacific Heights* to be reminded how awful that could be.)

Your son could refuse to sell the home when you want to move.

Your son could get in a car accident and end up with a lien on the house.

The house would now also be subject to claims in bankruptcy and divorce.

Just don't do it!

BETTER: The Beneficiary Deed

Leave it to Arizona to offer a brilliant alternative to placing your son on your home's deed. For a few hundred dollars you can file a beneficiary deed that provides that your house will go to your son when you die, still avoiding probate.

Your son has no right to the house during your lifetime. You have no risk from your son's irresponsible behavior. You can change your mind during your lifetime and cancel this deed. You can even sell the home with the son having no right to stop you.

BEST: Home Held in Trust

Even better than a beneficiary deed is deeding your home to your Trust. A trust offers the ultimate legal vehicle for control and flexibility. The terms in your trust determine who receives what under any conditions you set. You are the author of your own legacy.

BAD: Joint Accounts with Children

Some older parents will have their primary household account as a joint checking account with a grown child. The idea is that the daughter can pay bills or manage assets easily should she ever need to step in.

And just like with the house, because it is a shared asset, it does avoid probate.

Nevertheless, this is a terrible idea. If the daughter is in bankruptcy, divorce, or a lawsuit, these accounts are attachable.

And if you have a falling out, there is little stopping your daughter from taking the money and running. Even if you are getting along, there is nothing stopping your child from borrowing any time their own money is a bit short.

BETTER: POD and TOD Accounts

Your bank will allow you to have a beneficiary on file with a form that is titled "Payable on Death (POD)" or "Transfer on Death (TOD)." During your lifetime, the child does not have control of your funds. To access funds, the child would simply provide a certified copy of the certificate of your death along with their own legal identification and the bank will transfer full ownership to the child.

Of course, in the event of incapacity, the DPOA form should allow your Agent to handle your accounts on your behalf, but banks may want their own forms filled out ahead of time.

BEST: Accounts Titled in Trust

When you title your bank accounts in the name of the Trust, any purchases you make from the account are presumed to be held in the Trust unless titled otherwise. Your trustee would have access to these funds in times of incapacity or death and would distribute these assets as you determine, not as his own whims.

BAD: Automobiles Titled to Child

By now, you've noticed the trend. Don't share title with your kids. That is especially true for a weapon like an automobile, which is ripe for lawsuits. Just as with a house, if your daughter is co-owner, you are liable for her actions and she has equal rights with you over use of the vehicle.

BETTER: ATOD Form

The Arizona Department of Transportation has a beneficiary form that is free online that will allow you to transfer your vehicle upon death without being considered as an asset toward probate. Just print the form, sign with a notary and staple it to your car title. The beneficiary will have to bring the title, form, and certified copy of the death certificate to the DMV for a title transfer and will pay a small fee to get this done. If you change your mind, simply detach the form and destroy it.

BEST: Title Vehicles to Trust

Yes. It involves a trip to the DMV, which is nobody's favorite place to wait. But you can take your Certificate of Trust along with your title, ID, and check and change the title on your vehicles to your Trust. The vehicle will be distributed under the terms of your trust, but you retain sole control and usage during your lifetime.

BAD: Outdated Beneficiary Statements on Retirement Accounts and Insurance Policies

Retirement accounts and insurance policies are set to pass automatically to your beneficiaries upon your passing. The problem with these accounts is you often set them up, then never re-evaluate them. Often, your life changes but the forms do not. The wrong person can end up with your earnings. These distributions avoid probate and go directly to the beneficiary. There is often no recourse if these funds go to the wrong person. Many ex-spouses have taken full retirement accounts.

BETTER: Updated Beneficiary Statements on Retirement Accounts and Insurance Policies

At least every 3-5 years or with any major life change, you should look at your beneficiary statements. Remember, these will be distributed upon your death as one lump sum (or converted to their own accounts), but at least it will be to the right person.

BEST: Retirement Accounts and Insurance
titled in Trust or set as Beneficiary to Trust

When your Trust holds your retirement accounts
and insurance, the distribution pattern you set is
what applies to these funds. You leave your
legacy your way.

WORST: Fraudulent Conveyance

Every asset protection strategy here is designed
to prevent problems before they occur. Once
there is a problem, it is too late. It is unethical for
lawyers to transfer assets once there is a lawsuit,
divorce, or bankruptcy that might lay claim to
those assets. In fact, if there is a known dispute
that might lead to a lawsuit, it is already too late.
Attempting to move assets after the fact is a
fraudulent conveyance. This is criminal conduct.

It is too late to procrastinate when you are
incapacitated, sued, in bankruptcy, in a divorce,
or die. Asset and estate planning need to happen
before the crisis comes.

Chapter 14: Some Specialty Provisions

The Bimbo Clause

I once heard the story, probably exaggerated, of
a man who died leaving everything to his spouse.
She remarried and died leaving everything to her
spouse. This pattern continued 5 times until a ski
bum ended up with multiple family fortunes. The
kids from all these marriages were left with
empty pockets.

I know I'm in the minority when I say that my
spouse and I married young and had our children
together. My husband made $6 an hour digging
ditches and I made $8 as a clerk when we got
married. We had a boatload of debt and no
assets. Everything we've built, through
education, work efforts, and God's many
blessings, we've built together--and we've built it
for our children and grandchildren.

But I'm a realist.

If something happened to me, my husband would
have little trouble finding a new lady. He's got
washboard abs, most his hair, dreamy blue eyes,
and is a good provider. I shot and scored—and I
know it.

He would want to marry. And the likelihood is, she'd be younger than him. They may even have children together (my heart drops at the thought of that).

But what we've worked for shouldn't go to her or to those new children.

Enter the Bimbo Clause.

I'll admit that's a misnomer. And it is never titled that way. The idea is that 30 days prior to any remarriage, the surviving spouse's fiancé must sign a prenuptial agreement disclaiming all interest in the Trust other than incidental benefit during the marriage.

The surviving spouse can still use the Trust to preserve the current standard of living for the remainder of life. No new earnings have to be placed into the existing Trust. Anything the surviving spouse or fiancé earn after marriage is part of their marital funds and may be used as the couple determines.

Similar provisions can be added for unmarried children to require any future fiancées to sign a prenuptial agreement disclaiming interest in the trust.

Co-Dependence Prevention

Alcohol and drug abuse destroy lives. Unless a client opts out, I include a provision in Trust documents that keeps trusts from funding substance abuse. Basically, the clause says that if a Trustee becomes aware that a beneficiary is using illegal drugs or abusing legal drugs or alcohol, all payments received under the Trust are temporarily halted.

During this time, payments may be made directly to agencies that provide treatment and may pay for drug testing. Upon 12-18 months (the client picks the time) of a demonstration of drug or alcohol-free living, payments may resume. If there are required mandatory distributions that must be made during the treatment period, they are paid to a charity of the client's choosing.

Court-Challenge Provisions

You took the time to carefully create an estate plan, and now someone feels cheated. Your brother thinks he should be entitled to more than he's getting, or a disinherited child suggests that the relationship has been repaired and you just hadn't updated your plan. What now?

There is no will or trust that completely promises no one will ever challenge it.

But there is good legal advice. Give people just enough that they aren't willing to risk it if they lose.

One client gave two children about $500,000. Then two children with whom he had little contact over the last 20 years $50,000. It's his money after all. Can't he decide?

Sure. But that doesn't mean that the two slighted children can't file a legal claim and deplete the estate in legal fees which would be deducted from their faithful sibling's inheritance.

It makes sense to include a clause that basically says, if you challenge this, you forfeit what I gave you.

Some family members will take this at face value and walk away.

Some will disregard the clause and risk it all on principle.

Some will learn how the clause really works. If the challenge is successful: they win. But if they lose, they lose all—and have to pay their legal fees. A legal challenge is putting all their chips on the table, so the challenger better hold a strong hand.

A strong hand is usually going to be an argument that the parent was under "undue influence" of a sibling who had the will drawn in his favor.

It is even a stronger hand if the one who will inherit is not someone who would inherit under intestacy statutes (an unrelated care giver, a new lover, etc.).

To be able to create a legal challenge to a will or trust, the person must have been able to take a greater share under the state intestacy statutes than the current will or trust. Remember intestacy statutes are the legal rules of who gets what when there is no will.

One good legal strategy is to consider anyone who intestacy statutes would recognize and give that person enough that they are not likely to risk it in an expensive legal battle.

Chapter 15: Distribution Designs

This is my favorite part of estate planning. It is also the most time consuming.

I will ask you to tell me about your children, your pets, your dreams, your lifestyle, and your values.

I use what you tell me to form ideas about how you'd want to structure distributions.

A very typical distribution pattern is based solely on age. They provide health, education, maintenance, and support needs until a beneficiary is 25. Then at age 25 give 1/3, at age 30, give ½ of what's left, then the rest at age 40. This isn't bad. It will work if you give an independent Trustee discretion to provide for other requests.

The thought behind this typical pattern is that while a child may be financially irresponsible when young, she will mature. By the final distribution, she should be able to make it last.

Nice sentiment really. But it doesn't always prove to be true if patterns for more structured giving were not a part of life earlier on.

We can do better than that! Here's one example straight out of a client's trust (legal language included), but with names removed.

~~~~~~~~~~~~~~~~~~~~~~~~~~~~

I have created guidelines for my Trustee. These guidelines are designed for what would be a predictable life course for my children toward a comfortable and successful life path. These guidelines are not intended to shackle my trustees with impossible limitations, but are instead intended to build a framework that would enhance the success of my children. My Trustee is hereby granted the authority to use reasonable discretion to adapt or modify these guidelines for special hardships or changing circumstances that might include such challenges as managing an early pregnancy, becoming a single parent, making a career change, starting a business, dealing with the death of a spouse, or having a child with special needs. With an understanding that my true expectation is for my Trustee to use reasonable discretion outside these guidelines when needed, my Trustee shall administer the trust for each descendant as follows:

Distributions of Income and Principal when Beneficiaries are Under Age 18
~~~~~~~~~~~~~~~~~~~~~~~~~~~~

Our Trustee may distribute to the beneficiaries, the beneficiaries' descendants, or both as much income and principal of the beneficiary's trust as my Trustee determines is necessary or advisable for their health, education, maintenance and support. In addition, I make the following provisions.

My children must be allowed to visit and travel with my family members.

Furthermore, I recognize the importance of enrichment activities. There shall no limit on the funds that my Trustee may spend for extracurricular enrichment activities. Such activities include but are not limited to music lessons, sports activities, arts activities, clubs, classes, and summer camps.

It is important that money continually be invested during this period to ensure that college is fully funded.

In making distributions, my Trustee shall give primary consideration to the needs of the beneficiaries for whom the trust is established and secondary consideration to the needs of the beneficiaries' descendants.

Our Trustee shall add any undistributed net income to principal.

Specific Gift for High School Graduation

When my beneficiaries graduate from high school, it is my desire that each of them shall research, select, and receive the gift of a new car that is valued up to the equivalent of twice the annual gift exclusion (currently $30,000).

Distributions for College and Career Training

Our Trustee may distribute to the beneficiary, the beneficiary's descendants, or both as much income and principal of the beneficiary's trust as my Trustee determines is necessary or advisable for their health, education, maintenance and support. In addition, I make the following provisions.

It is my desire that my children have every opportunity to attend college to pursue careers that will make them self-sufficient adults under the terms below.

My Trustee should ensure that my children listen to a wide range of advisors who can provide perspectives on the importance of selecting a career path that leads to self-sufficiency.

The Trust shall pay for in-state tuition where he a beneficiary is a resident, as well as books, supplies, housing, food, and other reasonable living expenses as long as the beneficiary remains continuously enrolled in school (other than summers), including any Masters or doctoral programs. Out-of-state or private tuition may be paid only if the beneficiary has a plan or scholarship to fund the excess cost above the cost of attending in-state college. Should a beneficiary choose a path other than college, my Trustee shall help the beneficiary to establish a reasonable life plan toward a self-sufficient career path and guide them to demonstrate financial responsibility.

During the college years and summers, the Trust shall continue to pay for enrichment and extracurricular activities without reasonable limitation. However, these provisions cease upon graduation from college.

Routine Young Adult Distributions

When a beneficiary has completed all intended continuous education, payments for health, education, maintenance and support (HEMS) should be discontinued. At that time, the Trustee should instead pay an annual sum of the equivalent of the annual gift exclusion minus 20% (currently $12,000 or the equivalent of $1,000 a month). The first such payment will be treated by the Trustee and beneficiary as the end of the educational benefits in section (c) above.

The amount of the routine young adult distributions was chosen because it is not enough that it would encourage a person to discontinue work. I recognize the value of work and the importance of selecting a career that can be meaningful and profitable. However, it is enough that it could allow for a car every few years, a house remodel, or a continued pattern of enrichment activities throughout a lifetime.

This may be paid in monthly, quarterly, or annual installments at the agreement between the beneficiary and the Trustee. If the beneficiary completes college before the age of 25, the beneficiary may opt for these payments in lieu of HEMS payments. These payments shall continue regularly until the beneficiary reaches the age of 32. However, if the beneficiary should be in any court proceeding that would attach these payments, the Trustee may, in his or her discretion, resume making payments for HEMS in lieu of routine young adult distribution.

Funding for a Primary Home Investment

Recognizing the many benefits of home ownership, when a beneficiary has been able to live independently for two years, he may request in writing from the Trustee a 20%

down-payment for his first primary home. The beneficiary must be able to qualify for the home based on his/her own credit and must be able to demonstrate to my Trustee's satisfaction that the beneficiary can reasonably afford to maintain the home.

HEMS provisions or routine young adult distributions may still continue during the period that the beneficiary is "living independently" until age 32. The HEMS or routine young adult distributions are enough to supplement a living, but not enough to replace work.

Funding for a Business Venture

At any time after attaining the age of 30, the beneficiary may provide one business plan in writing to the Trustee. If the business plan has any potential for success in the Trustee's reasonable discretion, $100,000 from the trust shall be given for initial funding for the business venture.

Distributions of Income and Principal when Beneficiaries at Age 32

When a beneficiary attains the age of 32, the beneficiary shall receive 1/3 of the remaining trust.

Distributions of Income and Principal when Beneficiaries at Age 35

> When a beneficiary attains the age of 35, the beneficiary shall receive 1/3 of the remaining trust.

Distributions of Income and Principal when Beneficiaries at Age 40

> If at age 40, the beneficiary has children, he may take ½ of the remaining trust as his final payout under the trust. The remaining half shall be held in a trust for my grandchildren so that they might be able to attend college and be afforded the same opportunities as my beneficiaries.

> If at age 40, the beneficiary does not have children, the full trust shall be distributed and closed.

~~~~~~

As you can see, there is a lot of detail. This takes time to chat about and to create. This is part of the value of a Trust, which could never reasonably be accomplished with a will.

This kind of involved distribution design also requires that the person you choose as Trustee is
~~~~~~

equal to the task. You have to know that your
Trustee is willing to be involved with your family
for the long haul.

Chapter 16: Staying in My Swim Lane

When you network as much as I do, there are many opportunities thrown at you.

One of the most common is to sell insurance as many estate planners do. After all, insurance is critical in helping people protect what they've worked for. And why not make the commissions?

One big reason: it's not staying in my swim lane.

My business referrals are most often from Financial Planners and insurance professionals. If I'm stepping on their toes, I'm cutting off my own nose to spite my face.

On the contrary, I discuss insurance needs and make sure that my clients have someone who helps fulfill them. (Though I have a nice list of professionals who can help if my client doesn't already have someone.)

Similarly, I stay in my own swim lane on the estate planning products that I choose to offer my clients. There are a number of trusts that I do not offer.

Clients who have children who have special needs often need a Special Needs Trust. There is some science and some art to these trusts that takes extra care, caution, and study. I choose to refer these cases to attorneys who have built a practice in this area. If a trust like this is written badly, it could affect state and federal government entitlement programs.

Similarly, I refer clients to elder law attorneys when one spouse is likely to need state assistance for immediately long-term care. Planning between an insurance provider and an elder care attorney can make an enormous difference in whether the right trust will deplete a lifetime of savings or allow the healthy spouse to still retire in comfort for many years ahead.

Finally, if a client does happen to win the big lottery or have a taxable estate (currently 11.58 million for each spouse), I would bring in co-counsel with a specialty in the many trusts that minimize estate tax liability.

To put it simply, I won't offer something that I can't be sure will be effective to meet my clients needs. I want elated customers.

Chapter 17: It's Arizona's Fault

I'm a big fan of Arizona. Governor Ducey keeps leading our state in the right direction. Just this week, I saw an infographic that has our new state numbers.

Arizona is:
- #1 in inbound people moves.
- #2 in job growth (in part due to Ducey's act that allows licenses from other states to be recognized here for a number of jobs)
- #4 in economic momentum
- Holding our highest ever credit rating
- Proud that 175,000 have pulled themselves out of poverty between 2015-2018
- Building its private sector with 350,000 new jobs since 2015
- Experiencing the strongest manufacturing job growth in 30 years
- Holding $1 Billion in its rainy day fund.

And we get to enjoy sunshine year 'round!

But for all its praises, Arizona does have its faults. One of the challenges that I see here is the way the state is trying to remedy access to justice.

Lawyers are expensive. They took the long road to a high-end career. It is difficult for those of meager means to afford legal services.

To meet that need, Arizona has authorized Legal Document Preparers and LLLPs to act as attorneys in limited ways, like creating wills and trusts.

What blows my mind is that some of these folks with no more than a Bachelor's degree will advertise that they can create complicated documents like Special Needs Trusts and other specialty trusts. Even with a law degree, this is outside my lane.

DPs and LLLPs can network and market their services to anyone—they are not limited to those of meager means. People who have ordinary or even above average means can use these services.

People will get what they pay for. If money is truly an issue, I would rather see people buy Legal Shield insurance and go to a real lawyer than get a fill-in-the-blank DP doc.

As much as it depends on you, don't settle for the knock-off when it comes to your legacy.

Chapter 18: The Unethical Lawyer

I think every industry has a pet peeve. In
education, I hated to see the lecture method. I
was thrilled to witness active learning when
teachers used creative, engaging practices. I
could even share an article how using the lecture
method borders on unethical.

In entertainment, I hated the underhanded back
room deals that left talent with unmet dreams.

In estate planning, I hate seeing trusts that never
get funded.

It is borderline unethical to have a client pay for a
trust and go through the planning process and
then never let the trust own anything. It is
basically worthless paper that will now go to
probate. I've had several clients who had exactly
that before they met with me.

Industry talk suggests that at least half of all
trusts are never substantially funded.

One piece I do for my clients--I do create your
deed for your Arizona home (and other Arizona
real estate) to be placed in trust.

But the rest is a cooperative process between the lawyer and the client. Unfortunately, I can't go into your bank and ask them to transfer your accounts to your trust. (Honestly, I would, I think it would be faster for me to do it, but I can't.) But I can give you the pep talk the day you go to the bank and be on standby in case the bank gives you any problems.

I can email your financial advisor to send a copy of your Certificate of Trust and help fill out their forms for you to sign.

I can get on a third-party phone line with your brokerage, insurance agent, or place of business to request the right beneficiary forms.

And--no--I can't go to the DMV for you to transfer your vehicles to trust. (Even I have my limits.)

All of these tasks should be completed for your trust to be fully funded. If an attorney gives you a trust and walks away, that is at least arguably unethical. It will not serve the legal purpose for which you hired the attorney. Make sure that if you are willing to pay for a trust, you finish the job.

Chapter 19: Updating Your Estate Plan

There are all kinds of statistics floating about regarding estate planning. In 2017, AARP reported that 81% of those over age 72 have an estate plan and for those in the next age group of 53-71, only 58% have an estate plan. These numbers continue to decline in younger groups with the Gen Xers (37-52) at 36% and millennials (18-36) at 22%.

On a positive note, this says that there is no shortage of work for estate attorneys like me. On the dark side, it means that the state is going to be making a lot of decisions that people should make for themselves.

But what these statistics don't tell you is how many of these plans are current. It is not uncommon to meet with a retiree and hear that they haven't updated their will since they had their second child in their 20s. Their estate needs are certainly not the same.

This begs the question: How often should you update your estate planning documents?

HIPAA waivers are every two years. The others can last forever, but should still be reviewed every 3-5 years. If a provision no longer makes sense, it might be time to update.

Every once in a while, there is a major legal change that impacts wills and trusts. HIPAA in 2009 was such a change. And in 2019, the SECURE act affected inherited IRA distributions.

It doesn't hurt to sit down with your estate planning attorney to make sure your plan won't disappoint every few years.

In the same vein, major life benchmarks are important times to review your Trust. Here is a list of some of these life events that might trigger a necessary change in your estate plan:
- Having or adopting a child
- A large inheritance
- Marriage
- Divorce (yours or a beneficiary's)
- Child's 18th birthday
- Retirement
- Death or Incapacity of Spouse, Child, or another Primary Beneficiary
- Death or Incapacity of a POA, Trustee, or Personal Representative
- Change of Primary Residence
- Move to another State

- And with a Trust, any new asset acquired needs to be titled in the Trust or the Trust needs to be appointed as a Beneficiary

As you can see, estate planning isn't exactly one and done. Good estate planning attorneys will attempt to plan for all foreseeable events and have backup provisions for most of these events.

Every few years, just make sure that the document sitting on your shelf is still going to do what it was designed to do.

Chapter 20: What's Next?

Starting a legal practice in estate planning has been a crazy ride. Let's face it.
- Doing something I'd never done...
- In a place where I knew nobody...
- When I'd never run a business...

...that plan was just plain nuts.

But after studying the content, building a strong Phoenix network, voraciously learning about running a business, seeking out fantastic coaches, and getting involved in serving this community, I'm seeing the fruits of success.

It is not the kind of career that begs me to retire. If I want to be busier, I take on more clients.

What's coming? I'm working now on negotiating with a major cruise line to do game-based content to assist grandparents who need these services and services from others in my network.

I'm still enjoying my grandkids and sharing those joys on www.oursweetpickles.com.

I may be speaking on some stages with the likes of Loral Langemeier and Bill Walsh, as they teach people how to create and keep wealth. Trusts can be a wonderful instrument in that process.

I will always be building my network so that I can provide excellent referrals to other business professionals.

I'll be following developments in Domestic Asset Protection Trusts to offer one more great option to clients with more assets to protect.

And I'm learning to create content that keeps clients entertained as it provides educational value.

Stay tuned. As Bachman Turner Overdrive so eloquently put it, "Baby, you just ain't seen nothing yet."

If you're ready to Lifeguard Your Legacy, or if you are in a group that needs a speaker, please reach out.
- Visit www.lifeguardinglegacies.com,
- Call me on (602) 529-1827, or
- Email me – info@lifeguardinglegacies.com

I look forward to safeguarding your values-based legacy by earning and building your trust.